Building a Marriage of Substance

"Fight For Your Marriage"

———

REV. MRS. NAOMI ANTWI

Building a Marriage of Substance

Copyright © 2021 by Rev. Mrs. Naomi Antwi

All rights reserved. No part of this book may be reproduced or transmitted in any form or by any means without written permission from the author.

ISBN: 978-0-578-91921-8

Printed in USA

Dedication

To God Almighty
To my husband Stephen.
To my lovely children Aevya and Aeston.
To my dear mother Mama Mary.

Thank you all for your love and support.
I love you all.
May God Bless you.

"So then, they are no longer two but one flesh. Therefore what God has joined together, let not man separate"
~ Matthew 19:6 (NKJV) ~

Table of Contents

Introduction 5
Chapter 1 6
Chapter 2 36
Chapter 3 70
Chapter 4 104
Chapter 5 132
Scripture Reference 158
Author Page 167

Introduction

Genesis 2:18, "And the LORD God said, *"It is not good that man should be alone; I will make him a helper comparable to him."*-NKJV

Marriage was designed by God. God created man and decided to create a "suitable helper for him" Then God created a woman using a rib he had taken out of the man (Genesis 2:21-24). He joined them together as husband and wife and as one flesh. God created man and woman to have companionship, love, and intimacy. Many married couples have either forgotten, or neglected true companionship and oneness in their marriage. Many marriages are suffering from stagnancy and unhappiness because their marriage has lost its saltiness. Some have given up altogether.

Building a marriage of substance is structured to teach you the various stages of marriage, how to overcome the challenges that arise in each stage, and how to bring substance into your marriage.

Building a marriage of substance will teach you how to bring "salt" back into your marriage.

This book also serves as a guide for those engaged to be married, or interested in marriage. May The Lord bless you and your marriage as you read this book.

CHAPTER

1

The Four Phases of Marriage

Marriage is like a lobster.

When served on a dinner plate, it looks delicious on the outside, but when you try to eat it, you quickly discover that the lobster is not so easy to eat after all.

You notice as you try to eat the lobster, that it is actually hard on the outside and that the sweetest part of the lobster is the meat hidden underneath the hard shell. If you really want to eat the lobster meat, you have to take the time to remove the shell from the lobster in order to get to eat the delicious meat stuffed inside the shell. All the outward external things that onlookers see in the marriage represent the lobster shell.

Marriage looks beautiful on the outside, but when you get married, you come to realize that marriage is hard, and that you have to break through the hard shell to get to the happiness located inside the shell. The soft, delicious lobster meat inside the shell represents the true substance of the marriage.

Think of the soft lobster meat as the core of your marriage. The substance (lobster meat) is the rock that holds a marriage together. It is what keeps a couple standing strong through the storms of life.

Many marriages are failing because they lack that beautiful substance. Most couples give up on their marriage while still trying to "crack the hard lobster shell open", some get divorce the minute they discover that marriage is not the beautiful and easy union they envisioned. There's no doubt that marriage is hard. Successful marriages don't automatically happen. Money can't buy a happy marriage. It takes hard work to build a happy, healthy, and successful marriage. It also takes the grace of God to build a marriage filled with true substance. Think of it this way; there are four phases in a marriage. You need all four phases to work in conjunction with each other to achieve marital success.

None of the phases will work without the other. There has to be collaboration.

The four Phases of Marriage are:
1. The Honeymoon Phase
2. The Developmental Phase
3. The Crisis Phase
4. The Saccharine Phase

Each phase requires prayer, love, patience, humility, and most importantly the favor of God to be successful. Please follow me as we dig deeper into each phase on the following pages.

The Four Phases of Marriage

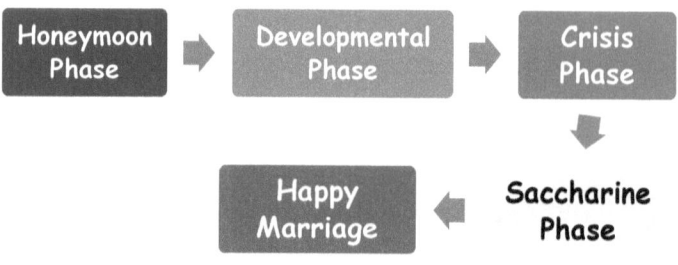

Let's start from the top:
"The honeymoon Phase"

1. **The Honeymoon Phase**:

The Honeymoon Phase consists of the most blissful times of a marriage.
Here, some couples go on vacation to celebrate their love. Others may not be able to afford the trip, but though they stay local, they still enjoy each other to the maximum pleasure.
These are happier times in the marriage. In this stage, the newlyweds focus on each other to celebrate their new life together. Whether a couple travels or not, they are madly in love with each other and can't keep their hands off each other. During the honeymoon phase, the marriage is in a state of euphoria. Wouldn't it be nice if the honeymoon phase will last forever?
Unfortunately, this stage eventually ends.

After the honeymoon is over, the marriage gradually transitions to the developmental stage. Some couples are blessed to have a longer transitional period, others are not so fortunate. For some, problems start shooting up during the honeymoon phase.

The Developmental Phase

2. **The Developmental Phase**:

The developmental phase mostly begins right after the honeymoon is over. This is time for the newlyweds to truly get to know each other. This is where courting for at least one year prior to getting married comes in handy. Premarital counseling also pays off big time in this phase provided the couple took the time to go through premarital counseling before getting married. Many couples conveniently skip premarital counseling, but that is a grave mistake that many couples pay dearly for after getting married.

I would like to strongly advise that premarital counseling is extremely vital for a couple during courtship. Without premarital counseling, many couple struggle. Some learn the hard way, and others don't survive that struggle.

Premarital counseling teaches the couple about what to expect in the marriage, and it teaches them good communication skills. The couple learns more about each other during the premarital counseling days. It also teaches them the different phases of marriage and how to deal with each stage. Premarital counseling doesn't have all the answers, but it does help greatly. It goes a long way in building and even sustaining the marriage.
My husband and I did not get premarital counseling prior to our wedding.

As a result, we learned a lot of things the hard way. It is better to be well equipped prior to going to war than to walk into a war zone blindly. If you are not married, it is important to invest the money and time into getting premarital counseling before you marry. Believe me; you will both be very glad you did.

Due to the fact that marriage is hard, and since marriage is a lifelong commitment, I suggest getting premarital counseling that is solely based on the word of God.

Bible says, "*All Scripture is given by inspiration of God, and is profitable for doctrine, for reproof, for correction, for instruction in righteousness, that the man of God may be complete, thoroughly equipped for every good work*"

- 2 Timothy 3:16-17 (NKJV).

As I was saying, the developmental phase of the marriage is "*the getting to know each other well*' phase. I know what you are thinking. You are thinking; "my husband/wife and I knew each other well before we got married. I do hope you are right, because, that will make all the difference in the developmental phase. Knowing your spouse extremely well before marriage will make this phase a little easier to deal with.

Let's face it, one or two years is not enough to know a person very well.

But it is enough to know whether or not you want to wake up next to that person every day for the rest of your life.

Most couples got to know each other for a couple of years before tying the knot. Some couples barely knew each other at the time of saying "I do".

The couple who barely knew each other will have a really hard time during this developmental phase, but with prayer, commitment, and determination, they will be successful.

The couple who knew each other well before getting married will benefit a little from this phase, because they will also have a lot more to learn about each other. The road can be rocky for them too, but they too will have success if they are willing to be patient, prayerful, hardworking, and welcoming to whatever erupts.

The developmental phase is where you learn the most intimate and some times, annoying and embarrassing habits about your spouse. I am talking about really knowing each other. I am talking about when the husband sits on the toilet in the morning while the wife brushes her teeth in the same bathroom; I am taking about the wife leaving her underwear and brassiere all over the bathroom floor after taking her bath. I am talking about the husband leaving his dirty dishes on the center table in the living room after the wife has cooked and served his food while watching Television.

I am referring to habits like your spouse farting and snoring badly with every turn while sleeping. One woman struggled with the realization that her newlywed husband started burping loudly in the presence of visiting family and friends.

Another person got annoyed because the wife had a habit of cleaning their teeth with toothpick in front of friends and coworkers.

A man got worried about the fact that his wife no longer attempts to put in the effort of looking sexy for him. These are things you may not have noticed about your spouse while you two were dating or engaged to be married.

The things you discover about your spouse in the developmental phase are nothing new, those habits, characters and behaviors has always been part and parcel of your spouse, and you are just now getting to know them better than before.

By the way, getting to know each other in marriage is never ending. It is an ongoing process because over the years you are both growing and changing both physically, mentally, and in some cases, spiritually.

During this phase, all the "masks" have been taken off and the real person (both you and your spouse) begin to emerge. Suddenly, almost every day comes with its own surprises. For some people, some of these habits are very disturbing, and others will see these as minor and "not a big deal"

This is the phase in the marriage where reality hits the couple that "hey, we are not dating anymore, we are truly married!" This phase reminds the couple that they are building a home and a family.

The developmental phase is also the "growth and adjustment" phase because this is when the couple gets to learn hands on about the good, the bad, and the ugly things about their spouse.

For example; most husbands discover that the wife's long beautiful hair comes off before bedtime and goes right back on in the morning because it's a wig.

In this phase, most husbands get to see their wife without makeup for the first time, and have to swallow the pill of whether her beauty still remains when the makeup comes off. This is the phase when a wife discovers that her husband prefers to go days without taking a shower.

This phase is the phase of learning new and in most cases, hidden things about each other. Unfortunately, this is usually the phase when a person finds out the hard way that his/her spouse is abusive physically or verbally.

If you are lucky, you get to find out about their abusive behavior before you marry them and hopefully run for your life.

The developmental phase teaches a couple each other's "true colors". Some couples don't make it through this phase. This is indeed a trying phase. The reason I named this phase the "developmental phase" is because, truth be told, it takes a lot for a couple to survive the trials and hiccups this phase brings into the marriage.

This phase is where married life truly begins. If a couple is able to weather the storms of this phase, the experience and knowledge they gain here helps them grow stronger than ever. This phase brings tremendous maturity. They say "what doesn't kill you makes you stronger". They grow together, and as you probably know, growth births development.

James 1:2-4 states, "*My brethren, count it all joy when you fall into various trials, knowing that the testing of your faith produces patience. But let patience have its perfect work, that you may be perfect and complete, lacking nothing.*"- (NKJV)

This phase helps the marriage develop new strengths the couple never knew was possible. It prepares them for the next phase of their marriage, which is called the "crisis phase". Beloved, if your marriage is in this phase, remember Philippians 4:13, "*I can do all things through Christ who strengthens me*" – (NKJV).

With God on your side, you got this! Make Jesus Christ the focal point of your marriage, and you will have a happy marriage.

Let's dive right into the "**crisis phase**".

The Four Phases of Marriage

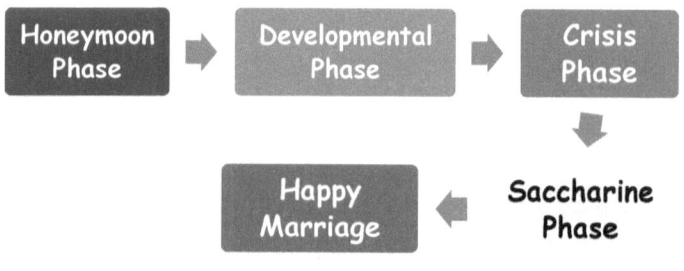

We are moving on to "The Crisis Phase"

The Crisis Phase

3. The Crisis Phase:

The crisis phase consists of all sorts of things. At this point, the honeymoon is over, the couple made it through the developmental phase, and they are ready for what comes next. This phase will go much smoother if the couple keeps their grip tightly on God. Keep your hearts on God's promise for you in **Isaiah 41:10**, "*Fear not, for I am with you; Be not dismayed, for I am your God. I will strengthen you, Yes, I will help you, I will uphold you with My righteous right hand*"-(NKJV).

In the crisis phase, the couple is still getting to know each other. Remember that the act of "getting to know each other" never ends in marriage. As my husband will say, "marriage is an ongoing process, and you have to trust the process"

"Trusting the process" starts with trusting God and trusting each other.

In the crisis phase, the couple is still learning to adjust to each other's flaws and adapting to marriage life. This crisis phase is also known as a "dicey phase", because many marriages rarely survive this phase. This is the phase that can make or break the marriage. During this phase, couples fight over the silliest of things and usually never recover from the minor misunderstandings.

This phase is where the marriage becomes stagnant. Sometimes everything seems boring because "nothing exciting is happening any more".

This is when one partner starts comparing how things were during the courting days to how boring things have become.

Some will communicate their true feelings and concerns to their spouse. Others will turn to a third party to voice their grievances instead of talking about it with their spouse. The crisis phase is when the couple will first have their heated, most dangerous, and hottest arguments.

When tempers are as high as they can get, no matter how angry you get at each other, it is very important to remember to control your tongues.

It is important to remember that though you may be very angry at the moment, you don't want the marriage to end. I say it again, please control your tongue. Because once you release those words out of your mouth, they are officially out and no amount of apologies will erase those words from your spouse' mind. Keep in mind that, once those words get out of your mouth, **you can't unsay it and they can't "un-hear" it.** Years after the argument is over, your words will come back to haunt you like a "ghost in love". Bible says, "*There is one who speaks like the piercings of a sword, But the tongue of the wise promotes health*" - Proverbs 12:18 (NKJV).

The goal is to control your tongue by controlling the angry words igniting inside your angry heart.

No matter how upset your spouse makes you, train yourself to think into the future and don't relish in the moment by saying and doing things that you will regret after you have calmed down. If you spit onto the ground, I think you will agree with me that you can't pick up that spit and swallow it back after changing your mind.

It is the same thing with your marriage, if you spit out words you should not even think about just because you are angry, it will be impossible for you to clean that mess up once the anger has subsided.

Beloved, a whole lot goes on in the crisis phase; financial stress adds it's footprint to the crisis phase. Family issues from either the wife's side of the fence, or the husband's side, can also make matters worse. Unfortunately, some couples lose a child at this phase of the marriage, and that loss understandably brings serious emotional chaos.

With such a loss, the couple must stick together, grieve together, and derive their strength from The Lord by praying together and trusting God for strength and healing. They should get professional help "as a couple" if needed.

This deep sorrow can either bring the bereaved couple together or drive them apart. The fate of their marriage after such a loss depends on whether they grief together, and confide in each other, or grief separately and confide in other people.

The shell cracking process officially begins in the "crisis phase" of the marriage; this is where the couple gradually removes the hard "lobster shell".

For every storm you and your spouse overcome together as a "**unit**" (Genesis 2:24), a small portion of the shell falls off. Every time you two patiently forgive each other, another small portion of the shell falls off. Hopefully, by this time, the couple has learned to stick together, and to depend fully on God – as a "unit".

The crisis phase is also the bonding phase because if the couple survives this phase, their experience draws them closer to each other in bonding. Their experience glues them together into "one flesh" (**Matthew 19:6**). The "oneness" in their marriage intensifies in this phase. If your marriage is going through this phase, derive your strength from The Lord. Prayer is the key. By now, every phase the couple has survived has prepared them for the next phase.

The "Saccharine phase" is worth the hassle and definitely worth the wait.

Bible says, "*But those who wait on the LORD Shall renew their strength*" - Isaiah 40:31 (NKJV).

Beloved, come with me to the "Saccharine phase"

The Saccharine Phase

We finally get to look at our fourth Phase called "The Saccharine Phase"
This is a very exciting phase.
I know you will love to hear about it.
Let's get right to it!

The Saccharine Phase

4. Saccharine Phase:

The Saccharine Phase is exactly as the name depicts, "excessive sweetness"

Yes, this phase is a phase loaded with pure enjoyment, love, and laughter. This phase looks a lot like the honeymoon phase, except it is way better than honeymoon phase, because you have been there and done that.

Beloved, if by the grace of God, your marriage makes it to this phase; you will realize that there is no storm you two cannot "weather", there is no fire you two cannot burn together, and there sure isn't any river you two cannot cross as a "unit".

It takes prayer, hard work, commitment, lots of tears, various heartbreaks, determination, and the fear of God to make it to the "Saccharine phase". You know the saying, "good things comes with hard work?" That is an understatement when it comes to the "Saccharine phase".

By the time you get to this phase, you have seen it all; you two have learned to accept each other's flaws, you have learned how to forgive each other, and how to resolve your issues without "airing your dirty laundry" all over the world.

Most importantly, you have learned how to love each other unconditionally.
In this phase, you two are going to take life easy and enjoy the "fruits of your labor"
The Saccharine Phase is the time you two get to enjoy the hard work you put into the life you have built together throughout the years. The Saccharine Phase is usually when the couple has been blessed to grow old together as a unit. This is when the couple gets to relax in retirement, enjoy their grandchildren (if any), and simply enjoy life together.

Here, they have more time to do the things they weren't able to do during their working days.

Unfortunately, many marriages bail out on each other just at the border between the crisis phase and Saccharine Phase. They give up when they are so close to the Saccharine Phase of their marriage. They walk out on the life they have worked so hard to build with their spouse. Of course, when they leave the marriage, they make way for some other man or woman to jump in and enjoy the fruits of their years of hard work. Then they start all over again with another person in another marriage.

For some people, the marriage cycle has become a pattern. They keep jumping from one marriage to another, repeating the same mistakes and yet expecting different results. Don't give up on your marriage, for better days are ahead if you just trust The Almighty God who brought you and your spouse together in the first place. Hang in there. Wait on The Lord, and God will renew your strength.

Don't try to do it alone, invite God into your marriage.

The Four Phases of Marriage

CHAPTER 2

Building and Maintaining Substance

Understanding the four phases of marriage will help you create and maintain true substance in your marriage.

The Four Phases of Marriage

What does **"A marriage of substance"** mean?

A marriage of substance is a marriage that is able to endure all of life's struggles, and still remain standing tall in an unwavering commitment to their relationship with each other, and in their relationship with God Almighty.

A marriage of substance is a marriage that has been grounded into the faith the couple have in Jesus Christ.

A **marriage of substance** is a marriage that has been built on the solid foundation of a godly marriage.

A marriage of substance is a marriage where the couple is prayerful.

Ephesians 5:25-33 has the blueprint of a successful marriage for couples to follow. In addition to the four phases of marriage listed in chapter one of this book, I personally recommend that you and your spouse take a few precious minutes to study and understand this blueprint.

This blueprint will help in building a marriage of substance.
Ephesians 5:25-33 guides you through the four phases of marriage, and makes the process a whole lot easier.

Be Real with Yourself

Creating and maintaining the substance in your marriage means having the ability to be real with yourself.

Be real with the fact that, as the years fly by, your man or woman is not going to be that same person you said "I do" to all those years ago; their physical attributes or defining traits will start to change, even their beauty can fade gradually no matter how hard they may try to prevent it from happening. Their character can change; some people get very impatient as they get older, others become more patient with age.

Be real with the knowledge that overtime, they will stop doing certain things they did for you in the past. For instance, they may have been opening the car door for you in the past; they might stop doing that at any point in time, and when that happens, don't get disappointed.

Life should go on normal. Don't expect that "breakfast in bed" to continue on a daily basis as it was during courtship, that will also stop eventually.

If you are lucky, they might surprise you by serving you breakfast on some special occasions. You should appreciate those some special occasions. A husband should be real with himself; he should keep in mind that if his wife had a sexy waistline in the earlier stages of their marriage, her waistline is prone to disappear when she starts having babies for him.

Only about 30 percent of women are able to keep their original weight after having babies. A husband has to come to terms with these changes and remain faithful to his wife. A wife has to come to terms with the fact that, even though the sex may have been awesome during the dating days and in earlier marriage days, once her man turns forty and above, he might need extra help in keeping up with her in the bed room.

She has to remain faithful to her man and work with him to bring joy in the bedroom. There are lots of medications for this kind of issues. Viagra is one of them. The couple must discuss together and the wife must keep this very fragile issue between them. There should be no reason to share such information with friends or family.

Apart from the doctor the husband might reach out to, no other human being must hear that her husband's machine is "temporarily out of order"

I know a woman who innocently told her male friend that her husband was having erection issues.

The reason why she told her friend this sensitive information was because her friend is an Urologist, and she thought he could offer some medical advice that could help her husband.

She said she went to him for professional advice on erectile dysfunction.

This action almost ruined her beautiful marriage because her husband was furious when he found out that his wife had revealed their bedroom secret to another man. He did not want help or advice from his wife's friend – especially his wife's male friend. It took a lot of apologies and prayers for that marriage to survive. The husband had to find a way to forgive his wife for what he viewed as betrayal. Seek help from a professional stranger if you must.

Be Real with The Truth of Life

Allow your heart and Soul to take all the unpleasant and pleasant changes in. Condition your heart to be tolerant. Pray and ask God to constantly renew and refresh your love for your spouse on a daily basis. Bible encourages us to "*ask and it shall be given*"- Matthew 7:7-8 (NKJV).

Believe it or not prayer works. You should try it. When we accept the reality of life, when we are real and truthful with ourselves, and we allow ourselves to come to terms with life's numerous little surprises in the marriage, we are able to find workarounds for our specific issues, and build a marriage of substance.

It is also necessary to be real with your spouse. **Honesty** is the key to building substance in your marriage. There is no doubt that the truth can really hurt sometimes and people don't like hearing the truth, but honesty is the best way to build true substance.

After all, the truth has a way of eventually creeping up, and when it does; your spouse will feel betrayed if they hear the truth from a third party source rather than from you.
Many marriages don't survive betrayal. Bible states, "*You shall know the truth, and the truth shall make you free*." - John 8:32 (NKJV).

Adopt truth and honesty in your marriage. The truth is always the best answer because when you are telling the truth, even if they wake you up from sleep your answer will never change.

Nourishing the Substance

Once the couple has successfully built a marriage of substance, they must work on "nourishing the substance"
Prayer must by now be part and parcel of the couple. One important thing the couple should be praying for, is to receive "the Spirit of wise counsel"
You might not be aware of this, but every married couple is in desperate need of "the Spirit of wise Counsel".

One of the most important duties we have as a married couple is counseling each other through thick and thin.
A man becomes more successful and well respected in the community, if he has a wife filled with "the Spirit of wise Counsel".
A wife who has been gifted with "the Spirit of wise Counsel" gives her husband great advice.

Bible says, "*The wise woman builds her house, But the foolish pulls it down with her hands*" -Proverbs 14:1 (NKJV).

Take Adam and Eve for instance, it was Eve who was deceived by the serpent (Genesis 3, 1 Timothy 2:14).

But Eve didn't go down alone, she advised her husband Adam to "join in on the fun", she managed to drag her husband down with her by convincing him that it was okay to disobey God and rather obey the serpent.

They both ate the fruit. Eve lead her husband into sin, and single-handedly crumbled their perfect home.

Because the serpent succeeded in deceiving Eve, and using her to deceive Adam, Scripture refers to women as "weaker vessel" (1 Peter 3:7). This is proof that a woman can easily become her husband's downfall.

As a wife, you should do everything possible to make sure that you are building your home and not crumbling it.

You can't do it by yourself; you need the grace and wisdom of God. You need God to bless you with "the Spirit of wise Counsel"

God put Adam in charge of their home (Garden of Eden) and God put Adam in charge of his wife Eve by making him the head of the family. Adam failed to live up to his responsibilities as "the head" by following his wife blindly into sin against God. Therefore, he was equally responsible for crumbling their home. Even though, God has made the man the head of the family, God still expects him to listen to his wife's counsel, but he must still obey God over his wife.

The man should pray for the "Spirit of discernment" from God, to know what advice to accept from his wife and which advice to ignore. A husband must never follow his wife blindly. The husband is strongly encouraged to constantly pray for "the Spirit of wise Counsel" from God, as he leads in the marriage. So that he also doesn't lead his wife astray.

If the couple has the ability to give each other good advice filled with wisdom from God, they are able to properly nourish the substance they have built in the marriage. Building substance in your marriage must be an ongoing process.

It's not a one-time thing. If you do it once and relax, you will not see the effectiveness of true and genuine substance. If you quit because "it's too hard" your marriage will fail.

Like any relationship, your marriage needs daily nourishment necessary for the substance to continue to grow, heal, and remain in great condition. As I have mentioned a few times, the two of you can't do this alone.

Prayer is the key. Please remember that prayer without action is futile. If you want things to change positively in your marriage, you need God in your marriage. If you want your marriage to move in the right direction, you need well grounded substance.

To get and to keep that substance, you have to be obedient to the word of God. God has given the husband a responsibility in the marriage and if the husband takes that responsibility seriously, God will stay in the marriage. God said that the *husband's responsibility is to love his wife, "just as Christ loved the church"* - Ephesians 5:25 (NIV).

God has also given the wife a responsibility, and she must also take her responsibility seriously in order for God to stay in the marriage. God commands the wife to *"submit to her husband as to the Lord"* (Ephesians 5:22 NIV). These are simple responsibilities that the couple should adhere to carefully.

For example, if you are praying for God to bring happiness into your marriage, and you go out and commit adultery or insult your spouse, or do things that would only bring war and confusion into your home, your prayers will become inefficacious.

You must change your heart, your mentality, your attitude, and your approach to issues. You must change the way you pray; instead of asking God to change your spouse' heart, ask God to change your heart. Ask God to give you both a renewed heart and love for Him (God).

When you both fear God extraordinary things happen. Continue pouring effectual prayers into your marriage. Ask God to step in and change things. You cannot keep doing the same things and expecting different results (that is just plain insanity). You cannot take matters into your own hands and still expect God to change things just because you are praying day and night. It is extremely important for you to practice the rules of God in your marriage. Having the fear of the Lord, creating unity between you and your spouse, being humble before God and each other, trusting God to help your marriage soar high in grace and favor, being patient with each other and with God, respecting each other in the most unique way, loving each other unconditionally, and loving God sincerely, and making communication the focal point in your marriage is paramount.

Faithfulness to your spouse and to God is significant. These rules are essential for the success of your marriage.
Marriage is very important to God.
I know this because marriage was the first thing God instituted in the beginning of creation between Adam and Eve (Genesis 2:18 and Genesis 2:24).
God said to Adam, "*It is not good that man should be alone; I will make him a helper comparable to him.*"
- Genesis 2:18 (NKJV).
It is important to note that this is the only part in God's creation that God used "*not good*"

God stated that it was **not good** for man to be alone. That is why He created Eve, to be a "companion and a helper" for Adam. It is noteworthy to remember that the very first miracle Jesus performed was at a wedding in Cana of Galilee (John 2:11).

Jesus and His mother Mary attended a wedding. There was a wine shortage during the celebration. Mary, knowing how powerful Jesus was, asked Him to do something about the situation. That was when Jesus turned water into wine. (By the way, I know those of you who are fond of drinking alcoholic beverages will be quick to remind other people of this scripture).

You have to take your marriage seriously because your marriage is important to God. Substance loaded with "the fear of God" is what glues successful marriages together.

FIGHT FOR YOUR MARRIAGE

There are so many women out there, yet God chose to pair you with your man as his wife. There are many men out there, yet God selected you to be the husband of your woman. As someone will say, "there are many fishes in the sea", but God chose you and your spouse to share a life together. That should tell you a lot.

One thing I am undoubtedly certain about is that when God speaks, it is final (Proverbs 16:1). I know for a fact that when God works, no one can undo what He has done (Isaiah 43:13).

That does not mean the devil will not try his very best to ruin a good thing God has put together. Satan will try his best by working through beautiful women and handsome men; sometimes he even works through children.

The devil will send a beautiful woman to test the strength of your marriage. If your husband is not strong enough or if he does not exercise self-control, that beautiful jezebel will become his side chick. And bam! Satan has found a loophole into your marriage. When that happens, "let the destruction begin" that will be the beginning of a very painful marriage, possibly even a divorce. For those of you asking what "side chick" means; side chick is a woman who is mistress to a married man.

The devil will send a handsome man (or as some women will put it, a "hot" guy) to test the wife's faithfulness to her husband and to God. If the wife lacks self control, she will find herself swimming in the devil's sea with the man as her "side guy" I am sure you have probably figured out the meaning of "side guy" by now, but just in case you haven't figured it out; "side guy" is the lover of a married woman.

This is another reason why it is important for a married couple to have a personal relationship with Jesus Christ, and to pray for "the fruit of the Spirit" They should pray together. Galatians 5:22-23, "*But the fruit of the Spirit is love, joy, peace, longsuffering, kindness, goodness, faithfulness, gentleness, **self-control**. Against such there is no law*"- (NLT).

Having "the fruit of the Spirit" helps you deal with any temptations the devil pours into you physically and spiritually.

Satan will always try, but you must be ready for him. Be Prayerful. Should your spouse fail to exercise self-control, and should they commit adultery, don't make the mistake of giving up on your marriage. Satan expects you to pack your belongings and bail on your marriage after infidelity occurs, but I challenge you to surprise the devil and his troops by staying put in your marriage.

That's right; the devil's goal for bringing infidelity into your marriage is to break the marriage. He is counting on you to leave and file a divorce so that he can make the other man or woman move in and take over your household.

They will destroy your spouse and your children. The best punishment you can give to the devil and his cohorts is staying in your marriage if your spouse cheats on you. Forgiveness is a powerful tool the devil will never understand. Let the devil's plan backfire by forgiving your cheating spouse.

A woman cheated on her husband. The man she cheated with wanted to get rid of her husband. He created a secret plan to break the woman's relationship with her husband. Unbeknownst to the woman, her "side guy" set up a scene to grab her husband's attention and to expose the affair to the woman's husband.

He expected the woman's husband to throw the woman out of the marriage so that he can have the married woman to himself. The "side-guy" succeeded in exposing the affair to the man, but he failed in breaking the marriage relationship. The husband's heart was badly broken and hurt when he found out what his wife had been up to. He was angry with his wife for the betrayal; he even tried to leave the marriage.

But his wife was remorseful and God stepped into that situation and turned things around. Suddenly, the husband felt the urgent need to stay with his adulterous wife. It took a lot of strength, and pain, but he forgave his wife and kept his marriage together. Their marriage became stronger after surviving what could've permanently sabotaged their home.

Beloved, if your spouse cheats, forgive him or her for their infidelity; cry if you must, be angry at them if that will help you with the pain they've caused you.

But when you are done crying and being angry, take the fight to your knees in prayers. Get down on your knees and pray like never before; ask God to help you heal. Ask God to bless you with the grace to go through the various motions of pain and anger the betrayal will bring.

Ask God to fill your heart with forgiveness for your spouse and the one they cheated with. Ask God to forgive your spouse and to draw him or her to Him (God).

Ask God to visit your spouse as He visited Saul on his way to Damascus and to have a supernatural encounter with him/her. Ask God to cause your spouse to repent and to create a loyal spirit within him/her. Whatever you do, please resist the burning temptation to fight the third party.

They are not worth the trouble. You have no business with them. Your business is with your spouse, your marriage, and with God. Whatever you do, please do not pack your belongings. Do not leave the marriage. Do not give up on your spouse. Do not abandon the home God has given to you. I started by saying that, there are plenty of people in this world, yet God chose you to marry your spouse. There is a good reason for that. Many people leave the marriage and file for a divorce.

They are awarded the divorce and they fall in love with another person, and get married again. In many cases, their new spouse may turn out to be worse than the previous one. Some people are fortunate to end up with a better spouse than the previous one. But not everyone get that blessed. You never know which side of the fence you'll end up. Instead of leaving the marriage, give it your best fight ever.

Fight with God as your Army Commander. Fight for your marriage with God marching in front of you, ordering your every step. While you are fighting to keep your marriage, do not withhold sex from your man or woman. If you are afraid of a possible sexually transmitted disease, you can politely have your offending spouse get tested first.

I am sure they will understand why they must oblige to your request. But if everything comes out normal, you should resume sexual activity with him or her. Withholding sex will only widen the gap the devil has instilled in your marriage. If you used to cook for them, continue cooking. If you used to do his/her laundry, continue doing that too.

The goal is to remain the same husband/wife you have always been. Don't change to become vindictive, vengeful, or "the punisher"

Do all the beautiful and sweet things you did prior to the adultery happening.

Do more if you feel like it. I say you should even go the extra mile and treat your cheating spouse extremely well. Let them feel bad about their action enough to repent from their sins, do this by showing them more love than ever before. There is nothing wrong with wanting to know why they cheated if that will help with the healing process.

After all, God has brought you two too far to allow the enemy to strip it all away. Fight for your marriage through forgiveness, prayers, and determination. I am not asking you to, "Do it for the sake of the children"

And I am not asking you to, "Do it for your extended family either"

Don't forgive because you are ashamed of what people will say if you exit the marriage. It wasn't those people that joined you and your spouse together, it was God who joined the two of you together and it is God who will continue to hold the two of you together.

So do not worry about the opinion of others. This is not about "taking one for the team".

This is about you, your life, your future, and your happiness. If you "do it for the children" or "for your family" or "for the team", you will be miserable in life and you will hate your spouse over the years even more. That action will hinder your blessings, and nobody needs that. I want you to stay in your marriage for God and for yourself. I want you to forgive and give your spouse another chance because God said so (Daniel 9:9). Do it for the life you two have built and shared together over the years. Do it because your marriage means the word to you. Do not vacate the premises to make room for the side chick or side guy to come reap what and where they did not sow.

Don't let the devil win. Don't give the enemy triumph over your marriage. I am not making excuses for your husband/wife's behavior.

But I do want to point this out; I would like you to keep in mind that some of these women and men, who go around breaking marriages and destroying families, don't do it by their own power. They are weapons being utilized by the devil. The devil is walking around "like a roaring lion" through these "side chicks" and "side guys" seeking which marriage he may devour (1 Peter 5:8).

Imagine this reality for a moment; why would a grown man, abandon his wedded wife of over thirty-five years for a side chick who was meant to be temporary? Why would he leave his wife and marry a maid-turned-side chick?

    And before you say "maybe the maid was prettier than the wife"

No she was not prettier than the wife. But even if she is prettier than his wife, beauty fades away and then character will be forced to surface. But that is a conversation for another place and another time. Why would a woman leave her husband of over twenty years for a side guy who has nothing to offer her? I know your answer is probably "sex". You are probably right to some extent. But sex is not everything. After the sex is real life. After giving up her whole life for sex, the sexual pleasure will fade away, and transform into a life filled with regret and pain.

You might say, "It happens" and you are right again. However, only a handful of married people might make foolish decisions such as leaving their well grounded home for a side chick or side guy. For the most part, many of these side chicks and side guys are using what Africans call "juju", and what some parts of the Caribbean and the southern USA call "voodoo" to charm married men and women and to drag them away from their spouses. Some usually target rich people.

But I guess everyone has their definition of "rich", so no one is safe from these people who have voluntarily sold their souls to Satan and his angels.

When it comes to these people, "rich" is relative. Don't relax because you don't consider yourself to be "rich".

What you consider poor, someone may consider "very rich".

Bible says, "*For we wrestle not against flesh and blood, but against principalities, against powers, against the rulers of the darkness of this world, against spiritual wickedness in high places*" - Ephesians 6:12.

This is why you should not walk out on your marriage. Rather, you should fight for your marriage. When I tell you to fight for your marriage, it is important to note that I am not referring to a physical fight.

There is no way to fight spirits with physical punches, curses, cusses or insults. You will be wasting your time and your breath. You will also be bringing a gap between you and God if you go out fighting and cussing or cursing people. Vengeance is The Lord's.

If you try to show your "macho powers" with matters of the spiritual realm, you will lose badly. It might even cost you your life. When I ask you to fight for your marriage, I am talking about fighting with prayers, prayers, and some more prayers.

Prayers will loosen, break, and tear down whatever the "juju" or "voodoo" may have tied up, or clouded inside your spouse' spirit. Some spouses voluntarily get themselves in trouble by chasing after men/women, and then, they get locked up in the devil's spiritual realm.

We have to be careful and not invite trouble into our homes.

Prayer will activate the power of God and all His Angels to descend upon your enemies.

Prayer is how we - Christians fight.

It is very important to remember that.

In fact, you and your family's life depend on the remembrance of this crucial fact – fighting through prayer.

Beloved, fighting for your marriage will strengthen the substance in your marriage. Remember, this is part of "the crisis phase" of your marriage, and you must come out on top and victorious. Hang in there.

The Four Phases of Marriage

CHAPTER 3

Strengthening the Substance

It is important to strengthen the substance in your marriage.

Sex is one way to strengthen the substance in your marriage. Sex is a beautiful and powerful exercise if it happens with the right person – your spouse.

There's no such thing as "too much sex" when you are married, as long as you two agree on what makes you happy. I have had the "sex discussion" with two married couples. One lady thought her husband loves too much sex.
She said her husband is "suffocating" her with sex. Another lady said her husband is not giving her enough sex.

One man is worried about his sexual relationship with his wife; he thinks his wife has lost interest in sex after the delivery of their third baby. He is concerned because he is a sex fanatic and he is trying hard to remain faithful to his wife.

Another man said his wife has been demanding sex from him every single night. I asked him why that is a problem, and he said that he prefers to have sex at least once a week and not every day. He explained that while they were dating, he and his then girlfriend, who is now his wife, had sex once a week.

But after having one baby for him, his wife's sexual appetite has increased dramatically and he can't handle it.
You see, everyone is different. You can't compare your sex life with your spouse to someone else sex life with their spouse. You and your spouse must know what each other likes and dislikes in the bedroom. If you have concerns about your sex life, it is extremely vital
to communicate those concerns to your spouse.
Communication is the way to
go. Someone told me that she really loves oral sex, but her husband hates going down on her. For this reason, she sometimes feels like turning to another guy to satisfy that sexual need.
Beloved, the best approach to strengthening the substance in your sex life is to simply talk to each other and find ways to please each other.
You belong to each other.

The day you said "I do" to each other was the day God granted you both a "Spiritual license" over each other.

Enjoy each other's bodies to the maximum fullest. Hold nothing back. When you engage in sexual intercourse, you are connecting your Souls together; you are bonding spiritually with each other.

That Spiritual bond strengthens the substance in your marriage.

Don't deprive each other of sexual happiness. Pleasing each other is all about being selfless. If he likes blow jobs, you give him a blow job, if she likes downtown, give her downtown.

Sometimes, you do it not because you like it, but because you love him or her. You do it to please your spouse. It's called compromise. To compromise is to be selfless. Selflessness strengthens the substance in your marriage.

Apostle Paul has great advice for married couples regarding this matter in 1

Corinthians 7:5, "*Do not deprive each other of sexual relations, unless you both agree to refrain from sexual intimacy for a limited time so you can give yourselves more completely to prayer. Afterward, you should come together again so that Satan won't be able to tempt you because of your lack of self-control*"

Well, there you have it. I believe Paul's advice is self explanatory. If you listen to him, it will help your marriage.
If you feel the sex is becoming boring between you and your spouse, don't turn elsewhere; Find ways to spice things up. Purchase books on sex, buy videos about sex, or hop on the internet for information on ways to rekindle the sexual relationship in your marriage. The internet has unlimited information on all kinds of stuff, it's amazing.
Take advantage of it. Major life changes such as menopause, pregnancy or illness

can cause a woman's desire for sex to fluctuate or disappear altogether.

Many people think that men are always in the mood for sexual intercourse, but that is not necessarily true. Some men struggle with low sex drive too. An illness, depression, certain medications, or stress, can cause men to have low sex drive. If you notice that you or your spouse has lost your libido, it is a good idea to see your doctor for the proper medical advice and treatment.

If you want the substance in your marriage to grow stronger, effective, and powerful, don't take sexual intercourse for granted in your marriage. I often hear some men complain about their wife's sexual behavior; some complained that during sexual intercourse, their wife "just lays on their back" in the military position, and makes no moaning sounds. These men are supposedly "turned off" by their wife's inability to show any action of enjoyment.

Some men complain about their wife's inability to scream and shout with pleasure during downtown exercise in the bedroom. This is their excuse for committing adultery with someone who will give them all the sexual sounds they want in the bedroom.

I want to give my brothers a bit of advice; if your wife is not showing interest during sexual intercourse, if she remains quiet and doesn't moan with pleasure while you are on top of her - that usually means that she is not feeling what you perceive as pleasure. If she is not screaming with joy while you are all over her, it means that she is not enjoying what you are doing to her.

It doesn't mean that she does not love you, and it doesn't mean that she doesn't know how to play along in bed; it just means that you have to "up" your game.

Has it ever occurred to you that maybe she is not the problem?

You might be the problem; she may not be enjoying the sex because you are not doing what you need to do to make her scream and moan your name out with pleasure.

Maybe, you are not doing a good job of meeting her sexual needs. Maybe, you are not doing enough to provoke a pleasurable moan out of her.

If she is not showing interest in enjoying the oral sex from you, maybe it is time for you to sharpen your bedroom skills. It's not that she doesn't know how to cheer you on in the bedroom; you aren't doing enough to boost her up to go crazy for you sexually.

No need to go cheat on her and no need for her to cheat on you either. Instead, talk to each other sincerely, be ready to accept the hard truth, and fix the problem rather than going in for a third party. When you are good at what you do, even a virgin will lose their mind for your touch.

Look within yourself and make some changes by educating yourself with videos and books on the topic.

She's yours forever, know your woman, learn how to please her, and learn how to fully meet her sexual needs. After decades of marriage, some men still haven't figured out where their wife's "spot" is and how to get her aroused. Same thing with some women, they have been married to their man for ages and they have no idea how to get his attention in the bedroom.

Beloved, this is a gigantic problem on its own. Fix this problem and substance will reign in your marriage.

Believe it or note, after communication and respect, sex is the third most important strength in your marriage.

It brings life and health into the marriage.

FAMILY

Bible says, "*For this reason a man shall leave his father and mother and be joined to his wife, and the two shall become one flesh'; so then they are no longer two, but one flesh.*" - Mark 10:7-8 (NKJV).

Remember, the man and his wife grew up in different families. In most cases, they both have extended families. When they become one flesh, their union is supposed to merge their extended families together as one big happy family. Unfortunately, this doesn't always happen. In fact, some married couples deal with a whole lot of challenges and stress related issues from extended family members on either side of the aisle. These issues, if not handled properly can break the marriage.

Whether the two families agree to merge beautifully, and to get along or not, **she** (wife) has to relate to **his (husband)** extended family and he has to relate to hers.

Together, husband and wife have to somehow rise above any challenges that may be threatening the existence of their marriage union.

DEALING WITH FAMILY

His Family

Most girls dream of their future husband since childhood. They envision this tall, dark and handsome man they will love to share their life with. They even plan out every minute detail of their imaginary wedding. Then they grow up and meet that man they have been imagining for decades. Everything is going well until they are introduced to his family.
Some women are blessed enough to automatically win the hearts of their man's family members on first contact; it's almost like "love at first sight"
Others are not so fortunate.
Unfortunately, they meet and marry this

great guy, but soon discover that the guy's family is a force to reckon with. The woman soon realizes that her husband's family hates her, sometimes, for no apparent reason.

To make matters worse, she finds out just how much influence they have on her husband and her marriage.

To help build, maintain, and strengthen the substance in the marriage, she has to find a way to deal with his family without giving them power over her marriage. She has to do this without alienating her husband.

As you know, everything begins with prayer. The best way to earn respect from your spouse' family is to prove to them that you have much respect for yourself; starting with the way you carry yourself, the way you talk to them, the way you talk to your husband, and the way you relate to them. It is vital that you maintain that mutual respect by not getting too close to them. You must love them from far.

They are now your family through marriage, but remember, the important keyword here is "extended" family.

So keep them "extended" by not hanging with them too often, don't go partying with them often, do not discuss your personal issues with them, and most importantly, do not under any circumstance, share your marital squabbles with them.

Once you cross the respect line, everything will go downhill from there. Be careful. Keep the relationship between you and them strictly cordial.

Her Family

Boys don't plan their weddings from childhood like girls do, but when they meet "the one", the possibilities are endless; they can fall deeply in love with that person. Everything goes well until they meet the in-laws. They soon realize that they've got their work cut out for them in dealing with her (wife) family.

As I mentioned earlier, to build or maintain substance in your marriage, both of you must learn how to relate to each other's extended family. Fighting with the families will only bring division into your marriage. The relationship between the husband and his wife's family must definitely be kept cordial. Respect is essential. I always say that if you show someone respect, it is impossible for that person not to reciprocate, unless that person is not considered a "normal" human being. It is the law of nature; it is the golden rule the Bible talks about in Matthew 7:12, "*Therefore, whatever you want men to do to you, do also to them, for this is the Law and the Prophets*" (NKJV).

Keep the "Extended" family relationship sweet, distant, and simple.
Keep your marital issues private and away from your family and hers.
You and your spouse will be able to strengthen the substance in your marriage if you keep these basic rules in mind when it comes to dealing with each other's family members.

SOME HARD TRUTHS

The truth is that, if your family loves you, they will love your spouse too. If your family respects you, they will respect your spouse. A family who cares about your happiness will not work tirelessly to cause problems between you and your spouse. Because they know very well that if a wife is happy, her husband is a happy man and vice versa.

They know that if they cause commotion in your marriage, hell will raise 24/7 in your home, and you might end up heartbroken or with health issues.

A family who is genuinely interested in your well being will want your marriage to succeed, especially if there are children in the marriage.

Here's a true life story; a man had a sister who was married with children.

Though his sister was married, the man was very close to his sister and he did everything his sister asked; he babysat her children, ran errands for them, etc. The sister's husband wasn't his favorite person on this planet, but he tolerated the guy and remained civil with his brother in law because he wanted his sister to have peace and happiness in her marriage. One day the man fell in love with a woman and got married.

His sister hated her brother's wife from the moment she was introduced to the family. She hated her brother's wife because her brother was no longer available to run her errands, babysit for them, or do anything else he used to do for them since he got married.

She silently held her brother's wife responsible for her brother's inability to service her and her husband. She secretly vowed to destroy her brother's marriage. Her tactic was to constantly disrespect her innocent sister in law.

The man remained close to his sister, but he was more focused on his own family. His sister was not happy with that. She found reasons to disrespect her brother's wife often and because her brother loves her, he often fought with his wife on his sister's behalf.

There was always a heated argument in the brother's marriage because the wife kept voicing out her concerns about her sister in law's rude behavior toward her. The man failed to see that his sister was intentionally destroying his marriage by preying on the love he has for her as his sibling. He kept dwelling on "I love my sister" and shutting his wedded wife out. He failed to uphold the vows he made to his wife on their wedding day, which was to "love, protect, and cherish" her forever. Soon the man's mother got involved in support of her daughter. They teamed up against the man's wife, the man continued to support their behavior towards his wife until he finally lost his marriage.

By the time he realized what he and his "family" had done to his wife, it was too late. His wife had left the marriage and was not willing to subject herself to such treatment any further.

One day, his brother in law disrespected him in the presence of his sister and when he retaliated, his sister teamed up with her husband against him.

This man realized that he had made a big mistake by giving his extended family precedence over his marriage. He realized that he had been the biggest fool ever, because now that the tables were turned, his sister never supported him against her husband when it came down to it. His sister took a stand for her marriage against him and made it clear to her brother that she loves her husband and he (her brother) better show his brother in law some respect for her sake.

The man learned his lesson, but it was too late for him to reconcile with his wife who was now his ex-wife. His ex-wife refused to give him another chance. She had moved on with her life and wanted nothing to do with him or his family.

Beloved, do you think this man's sister and mother cared about his peace and happiness? I don't think so.

If they cared about his happiness, they wouldn't have destroyed his happy marriage. But can we blame them?

Can we hold them responsible for the destruction of that marriage?

The answer, as unfair as it may sound to you, is simply "no".

The man is to be held accountable for his actions. After all, he is a grown man who claimed he was ready for marriage, and married someone's beautiful daughter, only to stand by and allow his family to maltreat and torment his wife.

In my opinion, he destroyed his marriage the minute he allowed his sister and mother to keep disrespecting his wife. I believe his actions encouraged them to run his marriage into the ground. That is what happens when we fail to properly prioritize. A husband and his wife were raised by two different families. God has brought them together in Holy matrimony. Now that they have become one flesh, their marriage union merges their extended families together.

Therefore, their goal should be to unite the extended families into one big happy family. This task is not easy to achieve, but it is not impossible.
The relationship between marriage and family must be prioritized. God must be placed on top of that priority list.
The order of priorities should be; God first, spouse second, children third, parents fourth and other members of your extended family come last.

Build substance in your marriage by setting the right expectations.

KEEPING THE BALANCE

You've worked very hard to build substance in your marriage. You defied all the odds or "so you thought". I told you earlier that marriage is hard work. If God has blessed others with successful marriages, He will surely bless your marriage too. But you must work for it as you continue to pray. Don't forget that faith and action must align with each other.

By the grace of God, you now have children. Children are blessings to every marriage, but we all know that the arrival of children changes everything in the marriage and in life. Children bring joy and fulfillment, but their presence changes the fact that life is no longer as you know and love. Once you have children, life is not about just the husband and wife anymore;

life is now about mum, dad, and the children. This is all exciting and fun. But how do you balance being parents, and being lovers all at the same time? How do you manage to keep nurturing the substance in your marriage? While raising the kids?

Many married couples go on a "slippery slope" when they become parents. Life swings 360° from revolving around them as a couple, to revolving around the children - as it should be.

From the moment the child is born until they graduate from college, every conversation the couple has is about the child. Conversations change from, "how are you doing honey?" to "how are the kids?"

Conversations go from, "I miss you honey" to "what are the kids doing?"

In most marriages, date night disappears and is often replaced with family dinner or family outing.

Some couples even stop giving each other gifts like birthday gifts, anniversary gifts, etc. Many quit acknowledging and celebrating their wedding anniversary all together because they are too busy celebrating the children's birthdays, school programs, and so forth. These things they ignore may seem minor, but I promise you that these things they are putting on hold are the very things that can keep the substance in the marriage.

Without these little things, the marriage will cease to exist and without the marriage, the children will not have a happy home.
So many couples put their marriage on hold and start building their lives around their children. There is nothing wrong with letting your life revolve around your children. The problem is that, the married couple soon forgets that they are in covenant relationship called "marriage"

They forget that it was this thing called "marriage" that started their family in the first place. They forget that God started this beautiful family of theirs by joining them as husband and wife in something called Holy matrimony. They forget that without that thing called marriage, their new family will cease to exist. They forget that without their marriage, their children will have a broken home.

It is very important to work on rekindling the love, closeness, and oneness in the marriage to keep the substance nurtured and strengthened while taking care of the children.
You may or may not be familiar with the word "multitasking.
The dictionary defines multitasking as *"the performance of more than one task at the same time."*
This word is often used at our various workplaces.

Multitasking is actually a great skill to have because it makes one an asset for an employer. In today's world, multitasking is needed in almost everything we do in order to be successful. That being said, *multitasking* can and should be easily transferred into our marriages.

As a mother, you are a teacher, a doctor, a nurse, a friend, a comforter, a cook, a beautician, a counselor, a coach, and everything in between. As a mother, it doesn't matter what mood you are in, how your day is going, or how you are feeling, you remain on duty 24/7 for your children. You do it all.

As a father, (hopefully) you are all the above, and then some. You also do it all. You see, you two have been multitasking this whole time as parents, and you probably multitask at your job every day. Why not transfer that wonderful skill into your marriage? Don't put your marriage relationship on hold any longer.

Strong "balancing skills" is desperately needed from both man and wife to keep the fire burning in the marriage while raising their family.

If you keep putting your marriage off to care for the children, by the time the children are all grown up, there will not be a marriage to return to. You and your spouse must make time for each other in the midst of all the chaos of raising the children, business, and whatever else life brings your way. Keep dating each other, over, and over, and over again. Keep talking about intimate things that matters to each other (other than the kids). Some couples have nothing to talk about; all they talk about are the kids. That must change.

Play love games with each other. Crack jokes, watch movies together, eat together from the same plate (by the way, this is a bonding exercise), spoon feed each other (it's amazingly romantic, try it, you'll love it!).

These are things many of you did while dating, you stopped the minute the ring went on that finger. This is a big mistake. Make love to each other after the children goes to bed. The goal is to keep doing all or at least, most of the things you used to do before the children arrived in the family. Definitely love your children. Be the world's greatest parents to them. Be there for them whenever they need you. But you still owe it to each other to keep the fire burning in your marriage (This is very, very, very important).

You owe it to each other to keep the substance growing strong and well nurtured in your marriage.
Don't forget that your children will not have a home without your happy and loving marriage. Therefore, balance, balance, and balance some more. Keep the balance between the children and your marriage extremely strong and steady. Top everything up with prayers as "icing on the cake"

Time to Decongest

The frustration, the tiredness, the stress, and the pressures of life can cause you to get upset about little things. Some women get irritated quickly during their menstrual cycle because their hormones go on a rampage, and their husbands suffer the consequences. Some men gets annoyed easily when their favorite sports team loses an important game, and they take it out on the wife. These things are part of life.

If you start feeling that way, allow yourself to decongest; pray about whatever the issue is. Go to the spa to release the stress if you can afford it. Go to the gym if you think it will help. After you get back to feeling normal, get with your spouse and talk about whatever is bothering you. Apologize if you have offended your spouse in anyway.

Make things right with your spouse. *Decongesting* is a necessary ingredient in releasing stress because it helps in keeping the peace and happiness in your marriage. It keeps you sane.

The Four Phases of Marriage

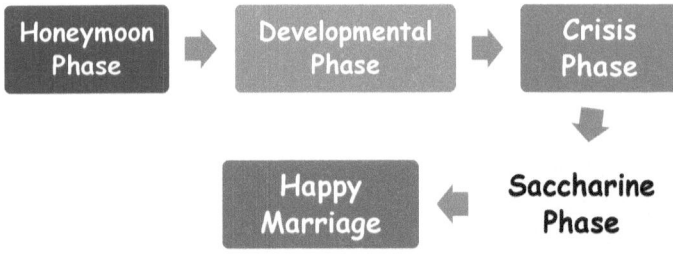

Two Imperfect People

CHAPTER 4

Two Imperfect People

I saw a sign that says, "A *perfect marriage is just two imperfect people who refuse to give up on each other*"
I couldn't have said it better myself.
I don't know who the author of this precious quote is, but I just love it.
The author is 100% correct.

A perfect marriage is definitely made up of two imperfect people who made a choice never to give up on each other no matter what comes their way. These two people did not only make a choice to stand by each other through thick and thin, but they follow through on their promise. Their minds are made up and nothing; no situation can change their decision.

Amos 3:3 asks an important question that is vital to every marriage couple; *"Can two people walk together without agreeing on the direction?"*

Beloved, the simple answer is no. Two people have to agree on the direction they want to go together as a team before they can successfully achieve that common goal. If you and your spouse agree to be each other's strength, each other's rock, and each other's confidant, you will be able to handle any hiccups or potholes you encounter through the years.

If you plant Jesus Christ at the root of that decision, absolutely nothing can separate the two of you.

Problems will come, misunderstandings will come, but you can overcome them together. Both of you have to make a choice to be happy. You have to make a choice to grow old together. You have to make a choice to forgive each other easily.

If you both accept the fact that you are *"two imperfect people"* who have made a choice to complete each other, you will be able to fully utilize the peace, love, forgiveness, and grace of God as strengths for your marriage.

This renewed strength will automatically deepen the substance in your marriage.

CHECKING THE PULSE RATE

One of the best things two imperfect people can do for their marriage is to periodically check how fast or how slow the pulse of the marriage is racing. I call this exercise "checking the pulse rate". You and your spouse have to set a date for this activity if possible.

This is the time of re-evaluating your marriage. This is the time to examine the strengths and weaknesses of your marriage. This is also a perfect opportunity to voice out any concerns or issues you may not have had the courage to bring up in the past (only if those issues are still weighing heavily on your heart).

It is a great idea to bring these issues or concerns up so that they can be resolved and re-establish the peace in your marriage. "Checking the pulse rate" helps you identify any "areas of opportunities" in your marriage.

Here are some examples of areas of Opportunities:

a. Are we both happy?

b. Are we content with our sex life?

c. Is there anything either of us would like to change about our sex life?

d. Is there anything either of us would like to do differently about our marriage?

Sometimes, you'll find that there are some detrimental unresolved issues that are still lingering around which requires immediate attention.

If there's unhappiness in the marriage, some vital questions must follow;

i. What am I doing that makes you unhappy?

ii. What can we do to bring happiness back into our marriage?

Once you and your spouse agree on what can be done to bring improvement, you have to come up with an action plan, and that action plan must begin with prayer. It can include making an appointment with a marriage counselor (preferably a biblical marriage counselor). The success of that plan requires commitment from both man and wife working together (Amos 3:3 comes in handy here too).

I said this earlier, and I will say it again because it is extremely important to **remember that** "happy marriage" takes hard work and prayer. It doesn't come easily. It's not as easy as it seems.
It takes **two**. If one spouse is not willing to even try to be happy, the other spouse will not be able to carry the burden alone. Most importantly, a happy marriage requires the presence of God as its foundation and pillar.

1 Corinthians 13:7 states that, "*Love never gives up, never loses faith, is always hopeful, and endures through every circumstance*"- (NLT).

If you are both willing, there is nothing you can't conquer, and there is no offense you can't forgive. "**Checking the pulse rate" of your marriage** a few times a year brings closeness, openness, and keeps the substance growing beautifully in your Marriage.

"Checking the pulse rate" is something I invented for my marriage years ago and it has been really beneficial.

My husband Stephen and I have tried this exercise numerous times in our marriage, and I can confidently testify to you that if done properly, "Checking the pulse rate" will work successfully for your marriage. I strongly suggest that you and your spouse implement this in your own marriage.

If you do implement this exercise, I would love to get feedback from you within six months to a year.

THE POWER OF MONEY

Money holds tremendous power to easily annihilate the substance you and your spouse have worked tirelessly to build over the years. The good news is that you two (husband and wife) hold a much stronger weapon over money, and that weapon is the power of "oneness"

As husband and wife, you have been united into one, and if you work together, you can get the power of money under your control and none of you will be slaves to money.

What I have learned over the years in my own marriage is that, a married couple is able to prevent money problems if they open a joint bank account and combine their money as a unit. Things work out better if the couple communicates to each other about when, where, and whatever they are using the money for.

You and your spouse can have separate individual bank accounts and save some money in those accounts, so that you are able to surprise each other with special gifts, and for your personal up keep.

But even with the personal bank account, your spouse should be aware of the existence of that account. If you keep it a secret, when they discover the existence of that account (and they eventually will), things can get out of hand really badly and very fast.

Some people prefer not to combine their monies with their spouses. Different people have different reasons for wanting to keep their money separate from their husband or wife's account. If you are a believer of separating your money and that decision is working for you, then that is fine. But I know from experience and from counseling many married couples that you are able to build and maintain a stronger substance in your marriage when you combine your money with your spouse' money. Things get even better if you are transparent and truthful about your spending. Get with your spouse and communicate about which method will work for you. Go with whatever method you two agree on. Whatever you do, make sure that your love for your spouse is much stronger than your love for money.

1 Timothy 6:10, "*For the love of money is a root of all kinds of evil, for which some have strayed from the faith in their greediness, and pierced themselves through with many sorrows.*" – (NKJV)

Don't allow your love of money to destroy what has taken years to build.

Don't give money and greed the power to separate what God Himself has joined together in Holy Matrimony.

Rise above the challenges of money with prayer, communication, togetherness, and determination.

Money is needed for many things in this world, yes, but money is not everything. Never choose money over your marriage or family. Money is replaceable, but it is almost impossible to replace a good, God-fearing spouse.

COMPARISON

One thing that can easily rip your marriage apart is comparison. One mistake people make is comparing their life to other people's lives. It doesn't matter whether they make millions of dollars annually, if they discover that someone else makes trillions of dollars, they want what that person has, and they will do anything and everything to either make trillions of dollars, or self-destruct while trying to get there. This behavior gets transferred into their marriage when they get married.

To effectively *build a marriage of substance*, you have to constantly remind yourself that no two people are the same, no two marriages are equal, and no two families are on the same level in life.

Even if it seems as if you are on the same level with someone, I promise you that you are never on the same level with anyone. This is because they can't be you and you can't be them.

You have been created differently. God has placed you and that person on different paths. It is better to stay in your lane at all times. You can't have everything you see in another person's marriage. What "wows" another person's spouse may not "wow" your spouse.

What another person's spouse may find beautiful, your spouse may find repulsive. For example, if you bleach your body because your neighbor's wife has light skin and you want to look just like her, your spouse might prefer black beauty, perhaps your skin color is one of the things he loves about you and that may be part of the reason he married you. Bleaching might bring problems in your marriage.

If you push your husband into buying a bigger and more expensive house because your friend and her husband bought a bigger house, knowing very well that you two are not able to afford it, foreclosure might become the basis for divorce in your marriage. Comparing another woman's looks to your wife's looks will bring unnecessary problems.

Badgering your spouse to "be more like" someone else, will drain any substance you have built in your marriage.

You can't build substance in your marriage relationship if you don't refrain from comparing your spouse to other people. It is nearly impossible to be happy in your marriage if you are not content with your life together.

Comparison causes people to be unfaithful to each other. Comparison makes you ungrateful to God.

By comparing your life to other people's lives, you are telling God that you don't appreciate anything he has done for you.

People who like to compare their lives to others are always miserable. People like that are not content with anything God does for them. Even if an Angel of God gets married to them, they will still compare their marriage to another couple's marriage, because they are never content with what they have. If you are serious about building substance, nurturing that substance, and maintaining the substance in your marriage, choose to be content and choose to be happy in your marriage.

Appreciate God and appreciate your husband or wife, appreciate your children if you have any, appreciate your career, appreciate your level of finance, appreciate your status in life, and appreciate your overall gift of life.
1 Timothy 6:6-9 states, "*Now godliness with contentment is great gain. For we brought nothing into this world, and it is certain we can carry nothing out. And*

having food and clothing, with these we shall be content. But those who desire to be rich fall into temptation and a snare, and into many foolish and harmful lusts which drown men in destruction and perdition"- (NKJV).

Beloved, enjoy every day as it comes. Make your marriage a Godly marriage, while adhering to your marital responsibilities.

MARITAL RESPONSIBILITIES

Speaking of marital responsibilities, don't use church to boycott your responsibilities as a married man or married woman. I have noticed over the years that some Christians use the church as an excuse to abandon their marital responsibilities. Some people use church as a convenient shelter to hide from facing real issues that are happening in their marriage.
Instead of addressing those issues with their spouse, they pretend as if the problems don't exist.

They deliberately get too busy with church affairs, and refuse to talk about their problems. They think those pending and growing problems in their marriage will somehow miraculously disappear if they just ignore them. I said it earlier that prayer without works is dead (James 2:14-26).

Don't think by diving into the work of God, and praying about your problems, those problems will vanish on their own. It does not work like that.

You must put work into resolving the problems in your marriage, as added incentive to the prayers. Some use Church activities to run from their marital duties. They are never home. They choose to volunteer for every church activity and every program just to stay out of the house.

For example; they go to their secular jobs Monday through Friday. They have different church programs or activities lined for every weekend; this weekend, they are travelling somewhere for the church convention.

Next weekend, they have to attend the revival at church.

The weekend after that, they have a church meeting that will last all day and they have choir practice afterwards.

When they are home during the week, Monday evening, they have to attend Bible study for an hour on the church conference line and they go to bed right afterwards. Tuesday evening, they have a prayer conference on the church line for an hour and half. Wednesday evening after work they have to attend a mid-week church service at the church premises. They come home late at night and go straight to bed. Thursday evening, if they are a church leader, they have a leader's meeting with the Pastor.

Friday evening they are too tired from all that back and forth and so they head to bed early. When their spouse wants to make love at night, they turn them down with the excuse of being in a "fasting mode"

When they do agree to make love, they are limited to what they can and cannot do in their marital bed.

Apparently, they can't do certain things in bed because "Christians don't do this and Christians don't do that". Some married people are using Christianity to limit sexual activity in their bedroom and this is ruining many marriages. A sex starved spouse will go and commit adultery with an unbeliever if that is what it takes. Don't drive your spouse into such detestable sin.

Beloved, Sex was created for **married couples**, therefore, being a Christian, should not prevent you from sexually pleasing your spouse in every way, shape and form. If you don't fulfill your duties, you will push him or her into all kinds of sexual sins.

Don't use Christianity as an excuse to become boring in your marital bedroom. Remember, sex was created to be enjoyed between one man and one woman who are in a covenant marriage.

Beloved, make time for your marriage.

If you don't, the whole time you are busy counseling and praying for other people, your home may be crumbling piece by piece because you are failing in your responsibilities to your spouse and to God.

You say; "How am I failing God when I have been busy with church activities and doing God's work, praying for others, helping the community and families?"

Bible states in Ecclesiastes 3:1 that,

"*To everything there is a season, A time for every purpose under heaven:*" (NKJV).

The fact remains that God considers marriage to be a covenant relationship in which the husband and wife both entered into willingly, with Him (God) as a witness (Malachi 2:14).

Man and wife chose their own date for a wedding, and they invited friends and family to come as witnesses.

Regardless of where they got married, they willingly appeared before God on that wedding day. On that faithful day, when husband and wife promised "to love, cherish, to have, to hold, for better, for worse, for richer, for poorer, in sickness, in health, and till death do them part", they made all these promises before God and they did this according to God's holy ordinance.

That day, God took those promises seriously and He expects husband and wife to also take them seriously, especially because they took that oath in His presence. So, while He loves to see His children devote their time to doing His work, and serving in His house (church), He also loves to see His children keeping the oath they made in His presence (Deuteronomy 23:21).

It will be humanly impossible for you "to love and to cherish" your spouse, and it will be impossible for you to be there "for better, for worse, for richer, for poorer, in sickness, and in health" if you are undependable.

You have to "be available" for your spouse in order to be able to fulfill those promises. You have to be present to be able to work out your problems. Abandoning your marital oath and soaking yourself into "the work of God" will disappoint God and fail Him and your spouse. If you truly want to live a godly life, if you truly want to please God, you can take care of your home and still do God's work.

Besides, you can't be useful to anyone outside of your home if you have problems weighing down on your heart from home. It is better to put your affairs in order at home and make peace with your spouse before you attempt to help others at church or anywhere else. Marriage is described in Malachi 2:14, as is a holy covenant before God. Therefore, marriage goes deeply beyond the earthly covenant the eyes can see.

Marriage is a divine picture of the relationship between our Lord Almighty Jesus Christ and his Bride, which is the Church. Marriage is also a spiritual representation of human relationship with God.

I want to echo the fact that God expects you and me to fulfill our marital duties and responsibilities at home.

Making yourself extra busy with church activities or anything else, will blow any substance you have in your marriage, or make it difficult to build any substance in your marriage. I know based on the word of God, and based on how God cherishes marriage, that God will not be happy if you use His church as a reason to push your covenanted spouse away.

Another thing you should consider is what Jesus commanded us to do in Mathew 28:19, He said, "*Go therefore and make disciples of all the nations*"

I will have you know that discipleship must begin at home. This means that you have to start by discipling your spouse, then your children, and then everybody else in the church and outside of the church.

Using the church or Christianity as a means to bring division into your marriage will defeat the purpose of discipleship (don't you think?).

Fulfill your God-given responsibilities in your marriage, family and then in the church.

If you want to create or build substance in your marriage, relate with your spouse in a way that greatly honors God's covenant relationship.

By letting the light of God shine through you in your marriage; your spouse will join you in doing the work of God, your marriage will flourish beautifully, and you will gain Favor with God.

The Four Phases of Marriage

Marriage is Sacrifice

CHAPTER 5

Marriage is Sacrifice

Apostle Paul wrote a letter to the church in Ephesus (Ephesians 5:21-33). In his letter, he described what a marriage should look like in a Christian home.

When Paul said the wife should submit to her husband "as to the Lord", what he meant was that the wife should submit to her husband's authority no matter how she feels about the situation.

Paul wasn't biased; he also told the husband to love his wife "just as Christ loved the church. He gave up his life for her" what he meant was that a husband has no choice but to love his wife no matter how he feels about the situation. Paul said the husband's responsibility is to love his wife no matter what she has or has not done.

As you can see, Paul was simply teaching both man and wife the importance of sacrificing "all" for each other. Jesus Christ showed mankind what "sacrifice" for true love looks like. I am not suggesting that you literally die for your spouse. I am reiterating that you must be there for each other even if it inconveniences you.

You have to give up the things that can destroy the happiness in your marriage. For example, if your drinking is causing problems in your marriage, give up the bottle. If you're a smoker and your smoking habit is bothering your spouse, quit smoking even if smoking makes you feel good. Sacrifice is an essential ingredient in building a marriage of substance. I have learned to let go of the less important stuff for the things that matter the most. You have to pick and choose your battles if you want a happy and successful marriage.

Don't start war over every little thing. You have to train yourself to be selective of arguments and confrontations in your marriage. Don't nag about things that will bring chaos.

The definition of a marriage of substance is sacrifice. Depending on how long you have been married, if you think back now, you will find that certain things that used to matter so much to you three, four, five, or more years ago, doesn't mean much to you in this present time. If you look back over the years, you will see that what would have been grounds for divorce for you seven years ago now seems petty and unnecessary.

Sacrifice in marriage is not about being victorious over your spouse (there is no win or lose rule in marriage), it's not even about who is right or wrong sometimes. It is all about winning together as a unit. How do you choose your battles? I have mentioned a few times in this book that problems are inevitable in every marriage. Whether you are a Pastor, a Deacon, Deaconess, Elder, Prophet, Music Director, Prophetess, church leader, usher, or church member, your marriage is no different. Your marriage will face problems. If you have not yet had any marital problems, you will. Problems are inexorable in every marriage under the sun.

Misunderstandings are inescapable in every relationship, and marriage is not exempted.

When problems and misunderstandings do come, it is important to ask yourself these questions:

a. Does this problem truly matter?

b. Is this problem worth fighting for?

c. Is this problem worth arguing over?

d. Is this problem worth the headache or trouble?

e. Is this problem worth dividing my marriage over?

f. Can I let this go without a grudge and bitterness?

If the problem is caused by a toxic friend, you have to ask yourself whether that friend is worth losing your marriage over.

For example, if your best friend takes pleasure in bad-mouthing your spouse all the time, if your friend likes to bad-mouth you to your spouse, if they are causing problems for your marriage, you need to evaluate the situation and re-evaluate that friendship, then you must sacrifice that friendship for your marriage.

Sacrifice your pride for your marriage. If you don't, it will be difficult for you to let go of things and to forgive your spouse when they offend you. If you allow your pride to get in the way of peace and reason, substance will not survive in your marriage.

You have to be willing to make necessary sacrifices for your marriage.

In other words, don't just make promises about sacrifice, just do it. If you are serious about bringing substance into your marriage, you must condition your mind, heart, and soul to bring your marriage first (after God of course).

One important question I want you to ask yourself today is;
 "In what ways do I sacrifice for my spouse?"
It helps to make a list of the many ways you make sacrifices for your spouse, and how often you sacrifice for your marriage. If you find that your spouse' list is longer than your list, you have some work to do. You should start that work with self introspection. Work on yourself and ask God for humility and grace to help you sacrifice more for your marriage.
This is a great topic to address during your "checking the pulse rate" exercise between you and your spouse.
This is also a great topic for your intimate spousal game day.

Beloved, marriage is hard. But it is also worth battling for. It is a blessing for a married couple to hit even one year anniversary milestone these days.

I have said it before and I will say it again, Prayer is essential.

There will be dark moments in your marriage. Every marriage goes through that, but that's not an excuse to bail on your marriage. On the contrary, this is when you should grasp tightly to your marriage.

During those dark moments in your marriage, when communication, sex, loyalty, respect, selflessness, and everything fails to work, Prayer is the key you will need to activate God's grace and favor for your marriage.

Don't give up; build the substance, maintain that substance, and nurture true substance in your marriage.

Fight for your marriage with prayers, determination, faith, and with good attitude. Pride has no place in a marriage. To build substance in your marriage, get rid of everything pride related.

All Queen Vashti had to do was heed to the call of her husband King Xerxes by presenting herself to him before his guests. The King just wanted to show his beautiful wife off to his honorable guests. Bible says the King "wanted the nobles and all the other men to gaze on her beauty, for she was a very beautiful woman" (Esther 1:10-12 NLT).

What Queen Vashti's husband wanted to do wasn't a big deal. He knew he married a beautiful woman and wanted to brag about her by flaunting her beauty before his guests. Some women might feel honored by this request from their husband and might even be flattered by the invitation. It wouldn't have cost Queen Vashti anything to elegantly stroll into that ballroom and allow her man to show her off.
Instead, Bible says that "she refused to come". Her refusal signaled disrespect.

This made her husband very angry, and brought shame to him and his officials.

Beloved, this move made by the queen was wrong and pure arrogance.

If you read the book of Esther, you will see that this arrogant and prideful move also cost Queen Vashti deeply.

This prideful move broke her marriage. This move handed her man and her crown over to another woman. Pride, arrogance, rudeness, and disrespect have absolutely no room in a marriage. These types of behavior are allergic to true substance and if you exhibit them in your marriage, substance will not be built or remain in marriage.

As a married man / woman, sometimes, you have to do something you probably see as "silly" for your spouse, just because they love it. Sometimes, you have to sacrifice your "seriousness" and do something "goofy" for your spouse, just because you know they love that thing.

You do things like these because you know that particular thing will bring joy to them. You have to sacrifice "pride, arrogance, rudeness, and disrespect" to have a happy and peaceful marriage built with true substance.

There is an old saying that "there are many fishes in the sea"

This means there are so many other men and women out there. This saying existed long before most of us were born.

It existed when home breakers, side-chicks, and side-guys weren't so popular. Back then, people who stole other people's spouses actually felt ashamed of their actions and therefore did that in secret until they got exposed.

In today's world, those people are proud of successfully breaking marriages.

They take great pride in taking another person's spouse for themselves.

They are so proud that they get on social media and brag about their actions.

In this modern world, "the human fishes have multiplied in the sea, both male and female"

Those human fishes are swallowing up marriages that would let them in.

Building a strong substance in your marriage makes it much harder for those fishes to sabotage things.

Your spouse sees all those fishes every time he/she steps outside the house. He/she is constantly fighting the temptations of falling prey to those sexually angry and lustful human fishes on a daily basis. With this in mind, you have to ask yourself, "What makes me unique from all those husband-stealing, wife-devouring fishes out there?"

The sacrifices you make in your marriage can influence your spouse when he/she is out there among the marriage-breaking wolves. The sacrifices you invest into your marriage today will make you unequal to those other women / men your spouse sees every day.

Someone will take a look at a happily married couple and say, "I wonder what he sees in her and why he's been faithfully married to her for so long"
Many people are wondering what you two are doing that makes your marriage so contagious, because they don't have deep access into your marriage to see all the sacrifices you two make for each other on a daily basis. They don't know what you have to put up with, and they don't know what your spouse has to put up with.
All they know is that you two seem happy together.
Marriage is sacrifice, and because any form of sacrifice is tough, many people fail to stay married for a long time. Sacrificing anything at all for another person is something a lot of people find very difficult to do. This mentality makes it nearly impossible for those people to stay in their marriage.

If you are not married yet, please don't rush into it. Take the time to go through Biblical Counseling. Learn about what it takes to build a Christian marriage.

If you are married, make sure you two are building your marriage with Jesus Christ as its foundational Rock and pillar. Don't try to do it alone.

REGRETS

Many people have regrets in their marriage. Some people regret getting married to their spouse for different reasons. Some has regrets over getting married to a spouse with low income. Some are frustrated over getting married to a spouse with poor credit history. Some are agonizing over marrying a spouse who has children from a previous relationship.

Some are regretting over accepting a marriage proposal when their hearts wasn't ready to settle down with that particular person. Some people are regretting over the fact that they got married at a younger age and wish they had taken the time to grow a little bit more.

They wish they had explored their options before finally settling down with one person for the rest of their lives. Some have regretted getting married either because they got pregnant or impregnated someone and found themselves in the position of having to marry their spouse due to that pregnancy. Some are having regrets over their marriage because they married their spouse thinking that they were marrying into great wealth, only to get disappointed after tying the knot.

Many people are unhappy in their marriage because they keep dwelling on the reasons why they should not have married their spouse in the first place. Some are living in regrets because they messed up in the past and do not know whether their spouse will ever get over their betrayal, or whether their marriage will ever be the same.
Many people have trouble building substance in their marriage because they have trapped themselves in the past.

They are not able to bring love and happiness into their marriage because they have imprisoned themselves in the "could have" and "should have" era. Bible says, "*Do not remember the former things, nor consider the things of old*" - Isaiah 43:18 (NKJV).

Whatever reason or motivation you had for marrying your spouse, whatever made you accept that marriage proposal, whatever you expected to get out of the marriage no longer matters.
What matters now is that you are married. Even though God knew your heart, He still allowed you to go through with the marriage for a reason. God does not make mistakes. Your goal now should be to do your best to make the marriage work. Maybe, you have not allowed your heart to love your spouse because you had ulterior motives for getting into that marriage. Maybe, you have not given your marriage a fair chance.

Maybe, you have not been putting any effort into building a real life with your spouse because you have always had one foot in and one foot out of the marriage. Maybe you don't have any ulterior motives.

Maybe your spouse did something to hurt you badly and you are still holding a grudge even though they think you two have moved past whatever it is that happened.

Bible says, "*Do not remember the former things, nor consider the things of old*"

It is time to forget the past. Pray to God for His help. Invite Him into your heart, and into your marriage. Allow yourself to fall in love with your spouse.

Start working on building substance together in your marriage.

Remember, the beginning of your marriage is not as important as the ending.

Obviously it is better to start your marriage with the solid rock of Jesus Christ as your foundation, because good foundation is everything.

However, if you didn't start the right way, it is okay because it is never too late for you to give Jesus Christ a seat of honor in your marriage.

After all, Jesus Christ said in Matthew 7:7-8, that if we, "Ask and it will be given to you; seek and you will find; knock and the door will be opened to you. 8 For everyone who asks receives; the one who seeks finds; and to the one who knocks, the door will be opened" (NIV)

Hold Jesus to His word and stand on His promises for you and your marriage.

DO SOME GARDENING

When we first bought our home, there was a beautiful garden in front of the house. It was obvious that the builder had invested a lot of time, and effort into that garden to make it so beautiful. The beautiful garden was part of the reason we fell in love with the house and that was why we bought it.

A few months after we moved into the house, the garden didn't look so beautiful any more. One look at the garden will tell you that it had been abandoned.

We failed to invest time or effort into the garden we loved so much when we first moved in. The garden eventually died completely.

Our neighbor on the other hand, takes good care of her garden. Our neighbor is outside every single day tending to her garden.

She treats her garden like her baby. And honestly speaking, her garden looks exquisitely beautiful. You can tell just by looking at her garden that she puts great effort into it.

Beloved, begin to see your marriage as a beautiful Garden. If you don't give your marriage the time and attention it needs to continue flourishing, it will start to gradually collapse and will eventually die completely.

Gardens that receive lots of love and attention tend to grow beautifully and are a joy to watch (like my neighbor's garden). It is the same with marriage.

It takes great effort to keep the love and joy alive in the marriage. It takes a lot of work to keep doing exciting and joyful things with your spouse. If you don't put in the work, the relationship between you and your spouse will stagnate and boredom will set in.

Plant Your Garden

Plant your garden in your marriage. Plant the things you would like to see grow in your marriage. For example, if you want to see unconditional love, plant unconditional love. If you want to see peace reign in your home, plant seeds that will sprout fruits of peace. If you want to be respected by your spouse, definitely plant respect by showing respect; for example, if you don't want your spouse to use profanity with you, keep words of profanity out of your own verbiage. Don't use **rude or offensive words under any circumstance if you don't want your spouse to reciprocate.**

If you want to see the Glory of God in your marriage, plant the fear of God in your marriage by being the first person in the marriage to fear God.

Be the prayerful spouse if you want your spouse to form a habit of prayer.

All these beautiful seeds you plant must be nourished constantly and consistently.

Proverbs 18:21 says that, "*Death and life are in the power of the tongue, and those who love it will eat its fruit.*"

Speak life into and over your marriage every day. Don't threaten divorce over every misunderstanding.

Don't talk foolishly out of anger. Some people cuss and curse and say all sorts of things to their spouse just to hurt them and by the time they calm down, they have planted so many emotional, psychological, and spiritual plants that cannot be undone. It is important for you to remember that you and your spouse have been united into one flesh in the spiritual sense. Therefore, your words can create deep spiritual dents into their

Soul and that can create a monster inside your spouse.

If you speak death into your marriage, death will wipe away your marriage and create darkness in the core of your marriage. Whether you are the husband or wife, whatever role you play in the marriage, make a promise to yourself to always speak life into and over your marriage no matter how or what you are feeling at the moment.

If you plant death in your marriage, you "*will eat its fruit.*"

And if you plant life in your marriage, you "*will eat its fruit.*"

Your choice; but if you truly want to create substance in your marriage,
I advise you to choose life and command life into your marriage.

These seeds must be maintained daily so that they will sprout into the ultimate substance in your marriage.

It all begins with you on your knees, it begins with you having the fear of God deeply rooted inside your heart, and it will continue with your ongoing commitment to the success of your marriage and your faithfulness to God.

SCRIPTURE REFERENCE FOR YOUR MARRIAGE

SCRIPTURE REFERENCE FOR YOUR MARRIAGE

When the problems come, when the tough times stroll into your marriage, and you have tried everything and nothing seems to work, do what you should have done in the first place; turn to the word of God for comfort, peace and tranquility.

During those dark times in your marriage, **remember God said**;

- I will be with you: **Deuteronomy 31:8**, "*And the LORD, He is the One who goes before you. He will be with you, He will not leave you nor forsake you; do not fear nor be dismayed*" –NKJV

- I will protect you: **Isaiah 41:10**, "*Fear not, for I am with you; Be not dismayed, for I am your God. I will strengthen you, Yes, I will help you, I will uphold you with My righteous right hand*" –NKJV

- I will be your strength: **Psalm 46:1-3**, "*God is our refuge and strength, A very present help in trouble. ² Therefore we will not fear, Even though the earth be removed, And though the mountains be carried into the midst of the sea; ³ Though its waters roar and be troubled, Though the mountains shake with its swelling.*"- NKJV

- I will answer you: **Jeremiah 33:3**, "*Call to Me, and I will answer you, and show you great and mighty things, which you do not know.*"- NKJV

- I have always loved you and will always love you: **John 3:16**, "*For God so loved the world that He gave His only begotten Son, that whoever believes in Him should not perish but have everlasting life.*"-NKJV

- When you feel overwhelmed; **Philippians 4:13**, "*I can do all things through Christ who strengthens me.*" -**NKJV**

- I will be your Guide: **Isaiah 45:2**, "*I will go before you and make the crooked places straight; I will break in pieces the gates of bronze and cut the bars of iron*" - NKJV

- I will provide for you: **Philippians 4:19**, "*And my God shall supply all your need according to His riches in glory by Christ Jesus*"-**NKJV**

- When you feel uncertain; **Micah 7:7**, "*Therefore I will look to the LORD; I will wait for the God of my salvation; My God will hear me.*" –**NKJV**

- When you feel defeated: **Micah 7:8**, "*Do not rejoice over me, my enemy; When I fall, I will arise; When I sit in darkness, The LORD will be a light to me.*" –**NKJV**

- Help to forgive: **Matthew 5:7**, "*Blessed are the merciful, For they shall obtain mercy*" –**NKJV**

- When you are attempted for fight: **Proverbs 15:1**, "*A soft answer turns away wrath, But a harsh word stirs up anger*" –NKJV

- When challenges arise in your marriage: **Micah 7:10**, "*Then my enemies will see that the LORD is on my side. They will be ashamed that they taunted me, saying, "So where is the LORD— that God of yours?" With my own eyes I will see their downfall; they will be trampled like mud in the streets*" –**NKJV**

BOOKS BY REV. MRS. NAOMI ANTWI

MARLORIE – GRACE UNLEASHED
By Rev. Naomi Antwi

Sovereign Insight: Strength for Your Marriage

By Rev. Naomi Antwi

Spiritual Enrichment: Daily food for your soul

By Rev. Naomi Antwi

ABOUT THE AUTHOR

Lady Rev. Mrs. Naomi Antwi is a humble follower of Jesus Christ, Ordained Minister of the Gospel, Author, Speaker, wife and mother. By the grace of God, she has been married to her husband Stephen for many years. They have been blessed with two amazing children.
Rev. Antwi is the Pastor at Spiritual Enrichment Ministries (SEMC).
Rev. Antwi and her husband Mr. Stephen Antwi host a program called Marriage Vitals for married couples every two weeks on YouTube and all social media platforms.

THANK YOU FOR READING

MAY THE LORD BLESS YOU AND YOUR MARRIAGE

www.ingramcontent.com/pod-product-compliance
Lightning Source LLC
Chambersburg PA
CBHW031250290426
44109CB00012B/516